THE JPS B'NAI MITZVAH TORAH COMMENTARY

Bere'shit (Genesis 1:1–6:8)
Haftarah (Isaiah 42:5–43:10)

Rabbi Jeffrey K. Salkin

The Jewish Publication Society · Philadelphia
University of Nebraska Press · Lincoln

INTRODUCTION

News flash: the most important thing about becoming bar or bat mitzvah isn't the party. Nor is it the presents. Nor even being able to celebrate with your family and friends—as wonderful as those things are. Nor is it even standing before the congregation and reading the prayers of the liturgy—as important as that is.

No, the most important thing about becoming bar or bat mitzvah is sharing Torah with the congregation. And why is that? Because of all Jewish skills, that is the most important one.

Here is what is true about rites of passage: you can tell what a culture values by the tasks it asks its young people to perform on their way to maturity. In American culture, you become responsible for driving, responsible for voting, and yes, responsible for drinking responsibly.

In some cultures, the rite of passage toward maturity includes some kind of trial, or a test of strength. Sometimes, it is a kind of "outward bound" camping adventure. Among the Maasai tribe in Africa, it is traditional for a young person to hunt and kill a lion. In some Hispanic cultures, fifteen year-old girls celebrate the *quinceañera*, which marks their entrance into maturity.

What is Judaism's way of marking maturity? It combines both of these rites of passage: *responsibility* and *test*. You show that you are on your way to becoming a *responsible* Jewish adult through a public *test* of strength and knowledge—reading or chanting Torah, and then teaching it to the congregation.

This is the most important Jewish ritual mitzvah (commandment), and that is how you demonstrate that you are, truly, bar or bat mitzvah—old enough to be responsible for the mitzvot.

What Is Torah?

So, what exactly is the Torah? You probably know this already, but let's review.

The Torah (teaching) consists of "the five books of Moses," sometimes also called the *chumash* (from the Hebrew word *chameish*, which means "five"), or, sometimes, the Greek word Pentateuch (which means "the five teachings").

Here are the five books of the Torah, with their common names and their Hebrew names.

> **Genesis (The beginning), which in Hebrew is Bere'shit (from the first words—"When God began to create").** Bere'shit spans the years from Creation to Joseph's death in Egypt. Many of the Bible's best stories are in Genesis: the creation story itself; Adam and Eve in the Garden of Eden; Cain and Abel; Noah and the Flood; and the tales of the Patriarchs and Matriarchs, Abraham, Isaac, Jacob, Sarah, Rebekah, Rachel, and Leah. It also includes one of the greatest pieces of world literature, the story of Joseph, which is actually the oldest complete novel in history, comprising more than one-quarter of all Genesis.

> **Exodus (Getting out), which in Hebrew is Shemot (These are the names).** Exodus begins with the story of the Israelite slavery in Egypt. It then moves to the rise of Moses as a leader, and the Israelites' liberation from slavery. After the Israelites leave Egypt, they experience the miracle of the parting of the Sea of Reeds (or "Red Sea"); the giving of the Ten Commandments at Mount Sinai; the idolatry of the Golden Calf; and the design and construction of the Tabernacle and of the ark for the original tablets of the law, which our ancestors carried with them in the desert. Exodus also includes various ethical and civil laws, such as "You shall not wrong a stranger or oppress him, for you were strangers in the land of Egypt" (22:20).

> **Leviticus (about the Levites), or, in Hebrew, Va-yikra' (And God called).** It goes into great detail about the kinds of sacrifices that the ancient Israelites brought as offerings; the laws of ritual purity; the animals that were permitted and forbidden for eating (the beginnings of the tradition of kashrut, the Jewish dietary laws); the diagnosis of various skin diseases; the ethical laws of holiness; the ritual calendar of the Jewish year; and various agricultural laws concerning the treatment of the Land of Israel. Leviticus is basically the manual of ancient Judaism.

> ➤ **Numbers (because the book begins with the census of the Israelites), or, in Hebrew, Be-midbar (In the wilderness).** The book describes the forty years of wandering in the wilderness and the various rebellions against Moses. The constant theme: "Egypt wasn't so bad. Maybe we should go back." The greatest rebellion against Moses was the negative reports of the spies about the Land of Israel, which discouraged the Israelites from wanting to move forward into the land. For that reason, the "wilderness generation" must die off before a new generation can come into maturity and finish the journey.

> ➤ **Deuteronomy (The repetition of the laws of the Torah), or, in Hebrew, Devarim (The words).** The final book of the Torah is, essentially, Moses's farewell address to the Israelites as they prepare to enter the Land of Israel. Here we find various laws that had been previously taught, though sometimes with different wording. Much of Deuteronomy contains laws that will be important to the Israelites as they enter the Land of Israel—laws concerning the establishment of a monarchy and the ethics of warfare. Perhaps the most famous passage from Deuteronomy contains the *Shema,* the declaration of God's unity and uniqueness, and the *Ve-ahavta,* which follows it. Deuteronomy ends with the death of Moses on Mount Nebo as he looks across the Jordan Valley into the land that he will not enter.

Jews read the Torah in sequence—starting with Bere'shit right after Simchat Torah in the autumn, and then finishing Devarim on the following Simchat Torah. Each Torah portion is called a parashah (division; sometimes called a *sidrah,* a place in the order of the Torah reading). The stories go around in a full circle, reminding us that we can always gain more insights and more wisdom from the Torah. This means that if you don't "get" the meaning this year, don't worry—it will come around again.

And What Else? The Haftarah

We read or chant the Torah from the Torah scroll—the most sacred thing that a Jewish community has in its possession. The Torah is written without vowels, and the ability to read it and chant it is part of the challenge and the test.

But there is more to the synagogue reading. Every Torah reading has an accompanying haftarah reading. Haftarah means "conclusion," because there was once a time when the service actually ended with that reading. Some scholars believe that the reading of the haftarah originated at a time when non-Jewish authorities outlawed the reading of the Torah, and the Jews read the haftarah sections instead. In fact, in some synagogues, young people who become bar or bat mitzvah read very little Torah and instead read the entire haftarah portion.

The haftarah portion comes from the Nevi'im, the prophetic books, which are the second part of the Jewish Bible. It is either read or chanted from a Hebrew Bible, or maybe from a booklet or a photocopy.

The ancient sages chose the haftarah passages because their themes reminded them of the words or stories in the Torah text. Sometimes, they chose *haftarah* with special themes in honor of a festival or an upcoming festival.

Not all books in the prophetic section of the Hebrew Bible consist of prophecy. Several are historical. For example:

The book of Joshua tells the story of the conquest and settlement of Israel.

The book of Judges speaks of the period of early tribal rulers who would rise to power, usually for the purpose of uniting the tribes in war against their enemies. Some of these leaders are famous: Deborah, the great prophetess and military leader, and Samson, the biblical strong man.

The books of Samuel start with Samuel, the last judge, and then move to the creation of the Israelite monarchy under Saul and David (approximately 1000 BCE).

The books of Kings tell of the death of King David, the rise of King Solomon, and how the Israelite kingdom split into the Northern Kingdom of Israel and the Southern Kingdom of Judah (approximately 900 BCE).

And then there are the books of the prophets, those spokesmen for God whose words fired the Jewish conscience. Their names are immortal: Isaiah, Jeremiah, Ezekiel, Amos, Hosea, among others.

Someone once said: "There is no evidence of a biblical prophet ever being invited back a second time for dinner." Why? Because the prophets were tough. They had no patience for injustice, apathy, or hypocrisy. No one escaped their criticisms. Here's what they taught:

> God commands the Jews to behave decently toward one another. In fact, God cares more about basic ethics and decency than about ritual behavior.
> God chose the Jews *not* for special privileges, but for special duties to humanity.
> As bad as the Jews sometimes were, there was always the possibility that they would improve their behavior.
> As bad as things might be now, it will not always be that way. Someday, there will be universal justice and peace. Human history is moving forward toward an ultimate conclusion that some call the Messianic Age: a time of universal peace and prosperity for the Jewish people and for all the people of the world.

Your Mission—To Teach Torah to the Congregation

On the day when you become bar or bat mitzvah, you will be reading, or chanting, Torah—in Hebrew. You will be reading, or chanting, the haftarah—in Hebrew. That is the major skill that publicly marks the becoming of bar or bat mitzvah. But, perhaps even more important than that, you need to be able to teach something about the Torah portion, and perhaps the haftarah as well.

And that is where this book comes in. It will be a very valuable resource for you, and your family, in the b'nai mitzvah process.

Here is what you will find in it:

> A brief **summary** of every Torah portion. This is a basic overview of the portion; and, while it might not refer to everything in the Torah portion, it will explain its most important aspects.
> A list of the **major ideas** in the Torah portion. The purpose: to make the Torah portion real, in ways that we can relate to. Every Torah portion contains unique ideas, and when you put all

of those ideas together, you actually come up with a list of Judaism's most important ideas.

> Two *divrei Torah* ("words of Torah," or "sermonettes") for each portion. These *divrei Torah* explain significant aspects of the Torah portion in accessible, reader-friendly language. Each *devar Torah* contains references to **traditional** Jewish sources (those that were written before the modern era), as well as **modern** sources and quotes. We have searched, far and wide, to find sources that are unusual, interesting, and not just the "same old stuff" that many people already know about the Torah portion. Why did we include these minisermons in the volume? Not because we want you to simply copy those sermons and pass them off as your own (that would be cheating), though you are free to quote from them. We included them so that you can see what is possible— how you can try to make meaning for yourself out of the words of Torah.

> **Connections:** This is perhaps the most valuable part. It's a list of questions that you can ask yourself, or that others might help you think about—any of which can lead to the creation of your *devar Torah*.

Note: you don't have to like everything that's in a particular Torah portion. Some aren't that loveable. Some are hard to understand; some are about religious practices that people today might find confusing, and even offensive; some contain ideas that we might find totally outmoded.

But this doesn't have to get in the way. After all, most kids spend a lot of time thinking about stories that contain ideas that modern people would find totally bizarre. Any good medieval fantasy story falls into that category.

And we also believe that, if you spend just a little bit of time with those texts, you can begin to understand what the author was trying to say.

This volume goes one step further. Sometimes, the haftarah comes off as a second thought, and no one really thinks about it. We have tried to solve that problem by including a **summary** of each haftarah, and then a mini-sermon on the haftarah. This will help you learn how these sacred words are relevant to today's world, and even to your own life.

All Bible quotations come from the NJPS translation, which is found in the many different editions of the JPS TANAKH; in the Conservative movement's *Etz Hayim: Torah and Commentary;* in the Reform movement's *Torah: A Modern Commentary;* and in other Bible commentaries and study guides.

How Do I Write a *Devar Torah?*

It really is easier than it looks.

There are many ways of thinking about the *devar Torah*. It is, of course, a short sermon on the meaning of the Torah (and, perhaps, the haftarah) portion. It might even be helpful to think of the *devar Torah* as a "book report" on the portion itself.

The most important thing you can know about this sacred task is: *Learn* the words. *Love* the words. Teach people what it could mean to *live* the words.

Here's a basic outline for a *devar Torah*:

"My Torah portion is (name of portion) _____,
    from the book of _____, chapter

    _____.

"In my Torah portion, we learn that_____
    (Summary of portion)

"For me, the most important lesson of this Torah portion is (what
    is the best thing in the portion? Take the portion as a whole;
    your *devar Torah* does not have to be only, or specifically, on the
    verses that you are reading).

"As I learned my Torah portion, I found myself wondering:
    › *Raise a question that the Torah portion itself raises.*
    › *"Pick a fight"* with the portion. Argue with it.
    › *Answer a question* that is listed in the "Connections" section of
      each Torah portion.
    › *Suggest a question to your rabbi* that you would want the rabbi
      to answer in his or her own *devar Torah* or sermon.

"I have lived the values of the Torah by _____
(here, you can talk about how the Torah portion relates to your
own life. If you have done a mitzvah project, you can talk about
that here).

How To Keep It from Being Boring
(and You from Being Bored)

Some people just don't like giving traditional speeches. From our per-
spective, that's really okay. Perhaps you can teach Torah in a different
way—one that makes sense to you.

> Write an "open letter" to one of the characters in your Torah por-
> tion. "Dear Abraham: I hope that your trip to Canaan was not too
> hard . . ." "Dear Moses: Were you afraid when you got the Ten
> Commandments on Mount Sinai? I sure would have been . . ."
> Write a news story about what happens. Imagine yourself to
> be a television or news reporter. "Residents of neighboring cit-
> ies were horrified yesterday as the wicked cities of Sodom and
> Gomorrah were burned to the ground. Some say that God was
> responsible . . ."
> Write an imaginary interview with a character in your Torah portion.
> Tell the story from the point of view of another character, or a mi-
> nor character, in the story. For instance, tell the story of the Gar-
> den of Eden from the point of view of the serpent. Or the story
> of the Binding of Isaac from the point of view of the ram, which
> was substituted for Isaac as a sacrifice. Or perhaps the story of
> the sale of Joseph from the point of view of his coat, which was
> stripped off him and dipped in a goat's blood.
> Write a poem about your Torah portion.
> Write a song about your Torah portion.
> Write a play about your Torah portion, and have some friends act
> it out with you.
> Create a piece of artwork about your Torah portion.

The bottom line is: Make this a joyful experience. Yes—it could
even be fun.

The Very Last Thing You Need to Know at This Point

The Torah scroll is written without vowels. Why? Don't *sofrim* (Torah scribes) know the vowels?

Of course they do.

So, why do they leave the vowels out?

One reason is that the Torah came into existence at a time when sages were still arguing about the proper vowels, and the proper pronunciation.

But here is another reason: The Torah text, as we have it today, and as it sits in the scroll, is actually *an unfinished work*. Think of it: the words are just sitting there. Because they have no vowels, it is as if they have no voice.

When we read the Torah publicly, we give voice to the ancient words. And when we find meaning in those ancient words, and we talk about those meanings, those words jump to life. They enter our lives. They make our world deeper and better.

Mazal tov to you, and your family. This is your journey toward Jewish maturity. Love it.

THE TORAH

❖ Bere'shit: Genesis 1:1–6:8

This is how it all starts—with a Torah portion that poses a lot of questions. God creates the world in six days (right, but how long was a day?). God rests on the seventh day, which is how Shabbat gets started. God then creates Adam and Eve and places them in the Garden of Eden.

Things are going great until Adam and Eve disobey God by eating from the Tree of Knowledge of Good and Evil. God kicks them out of the garden. Just when you think things are bad enough, Cain kills his brother, Abel. As punishment, Cain is condemned to wander the earth. And over the next several generations, humanity increasingly descends into violence.

Maybe the whole "humanity" project isn't working out as well as God had planned. Stay tuned for God's solution to the problem.

Summary

- ‣ God creates the universe as we know it in a series of six days. (1:1–29)
- ‣ Human beings are created in the image of God. (1:26–28)
- ‣ The seventh day of creation is a day of rest—Shabbat—and God declares it holy. (2:1–3)
- ‣ Human beings had a special role in the Garden of Eden, and God commands them not to eat from the Tree of Knowledge of Good and Evil. The snake convinces Adam and Eve to disobey God's command, with severe consequences that include expulsion from the garden. (2:4–3:24)
- ‣ Cain kills his brother, Abel, and God confronts him. From there, things go downhill fast and humanity increasingly descends into violence. (4:1–6:8)

The Big Ideas

- **The story of creation in Genesis is a moral story, about the nature of the world and of humanity itself.** It contains ethical teachings about the pattern of creation and the meaning of the world itself.

- **God created order out of chaos.** We don't know how long a day was, but the most important thing is that there is a rhythm and pattern to creation, and that things do not simply happen in a random way.

- **Language is a tool of creation.** That is precisely how God uses language: "Let there be . . ." The words that we say have the power to create worlds, or, if we use words irresponsibly, they can destroy worlds—and people—as well.

- **Nature must be respected.** We are not free to do whatever we want to the earth, its living things, and its resources. Because the earth is God's creation, we must respect it and take care of it, which was one of God's commandments to Adam and Eve in the Garden of Eden.

- **Special times can be holy.** The first thing declared holy in the Torah is not a place nor a person, but a time. The seventh day is holy and set apart because God rested on that day. When we rest on Shabbat we too make it a holy—a special—day.

- **Human beings are responsible for one another.** The Torah tells us that humanity is made in God's image, and one way of interpreting this is that there is a piece of God within us all. In some deep way, we are all connected to each other and to God, and we should treat one other as we want to be treated, and as God would want to be treated.

Divrei Torah

IN GOD'S IMAGE: WHAT DOES IT MEAN?

The last thing that God creates is humanity. The Torah suggests that perhaps God saved the best for last. We are uniquely described as created in God's image: "And God created humankind in the divine image, creating it in the image of God—creating them male and female" (1:27).

This is perhaps the greatest idea that Judaism ever gave to the world—that every person has the spark of divinity within him or her. The great sage Rabbi Akiba recognized that our awareness of this spark makes us even more special: "Beloved are human beings, because they were created in the divine image. But it was through a special love that they became aware that they were created in the divine image."

What does this really mean—"in the divine image"?

On its most basic level, it means that while we are certainly not God, in some way we resemble God. It means that we should try to imitate God. A large part of our human responsibilities flow from the various things that God does in the Torah. Our tradition teaches that as God creates, we can create. As God clothes Adam and Eve, so we can clothe the needy. As God gives life, so we strive to heal the sick.

Being made in God's image means that we have special tasks and opportunities in the world. We have a special responsibility to care for all of God's creation. Because God created the world and all living things within it, we must avoid destruction of the earth and its plant life (*ba'al tashhit*). Because God created *and blessed* animals (1:22), we must avoid cruelty to animals (*tza'ar ba'alei chayyim*). Because God created, blessed, *and* made human beings in the divine image, we must recognize the sacred in all human beings and cherish them. Yes, to avoid destruction, and yes, to avoid cruelty—but also to create ways of helping people through acts of kindness (*gemilut chasadim*).

Note that the Torah teaches that both man *and* woman are made in the divine image. All people are equal in dignity and deserve equal respect and opportunity. In the words of Rabbi Irving (Yitz) Greenberg, in an imitation of the American Declaration of Independence, which also speaks of basic rights: "We hold these truths to be self-evident: that all human beings are created in the image of God, that they are endowed by their Creator with certain fundamental dignities, that among these are infinite value, equality and uniqueness. Our faith calls on all humanity to join in a covenant with God and a partnership between the generations for *tikkun olam* (the repair of the world) so that all forms of life are sustained in the fullest of dignity."

So, that is the Jewish task: to work toward a world where everyone knows that he or she is created in the divine image. And a world where everyone else knows it as well!

WHERE IS YOUR BROTHER?

In one sense, Cain was the first and worst murderer in the world. When he killed his brother, Abel, he essentially wiped out one-quarter of all humanity, because the Torah claims that at that time there were only four people in the world: Adam, Eve, Cain, and Abel.

Both Cain and Abel brought offerings to God. God accepted Abel's offering of a lamb, but rejected Cain's offering of grain. Cain is very jealous, and very angry.

God warned Cain that "sin crouches at the door"—that we have to be careful of our feelings of anger and jealousy. It was too late for Cain to engage in "anger management." Cain killed Abel. God asked Cain: "Where is your brother Abel?" (4:9). To which Cain responded: "I don't know. Am I my brother's keeper?"

Of course, God knew where Abel was. (God is, after all, God, who knows everything.) God simply wanted Cain to own up to what he had done, and to learn the lesson of moral responsibility.

More than this: God wanted Cain to know that he had not only killed Abel. The text says that Abel's bloods (*demei*) cried out from the ground—a strange way of putting it, especially since "blood" is one of those words that has no plural form. A midrash explains it this way: "It is not written, 'Your brother's blood cries out to me from the ground!' but 'your brother's *bloods*'—not only his blood, but also the blood of his descendants."

The tragedy of it all is that Cain not only took his brother's life, but also cut off his brother's line forever, and then evaded responsibility.

God spared Cain's life, however, while putting a mark on him. One wonders: Did Cain learn his lesson in any way? As Rabbi Marshall Meyer said: "True hope is born when I learn to scream NO to injustice, to bribery, to corruption; when I scream that I will be involved; when I scream that I won't stay frozen in my ways. True hope is born when I can scream with all my being: YES to honesty; YES, I am my brother's keeper!"

Connections

- In many places in the United States, people think that schools should teach the biblical version of creation, as well as the theory of evolution. How do you feel about this?
- Why is Shabbat important to the Jewish people? Is it important to you and your family? How do you make it so? What do you think an ideal Shabbat would be like?
- What does being created in the divine image mean to you? What are some examples of ways that we can show that people are made in the divine image?
- What are some of the implications of the way that we are supposed to care for the earth? For animals? Is it a violation of *tza'ar ba'alei chayyim* (avoid cruelty to animals) to experiment on animals for medical research? What about for cosmetic research?
- We might think of the entire Torah as the answer to God's question to Cain: "Where is Abel your brother?" What are some ways this is so?

THE HAFTARAH

❖ Bere'shit: Isaiah 42:5–43:10

There is no time like the very beginning of the Torah reading cycle to remember exactly why we Jews have to do what we do.

But, first, let's clear up a little confusion. There were two prophets named Isaiah. The first one preached in the Southern Kingdom of Judah in the second half of the eighth century BCE. The second one, usually called Second Isaiah, was actually an anonymous prophet who preached during the sixth century BCE during the Babylonian exile. (A little history lesson: in the year 586 BCE, Babylonian armies destroyed Jerusalem, burned the Temple, and deported the Judeans to Babylonia, thus beginning the period known as the Babylonian exile.) Actually, the second prophet's name wasn't really Isaiah; someone simply added his teachings to the end of the book of the original Isaiah.

The prophet known as Second Isaiah delivered a speech to the Judeans who were in exile in Babylonia, and in it he reminds them that while God is the creator of the earth (which is the connection to the Torah portion Bere'shit), God also has a direct, loving, and personal relationship with the Jewish people.

"A Light to the Nations"

Along with this relationship comes a special responsibility—the Jewish people are to be, in the memorable language of Isaiah, a "covenant people" and "a light of nations." To be "a light of nations" means that the Jews have a responsibility not only to themselves, but to the world as well. These obligations are not ritual obligations; it is not that the Jews have to go to other peoples and talk to them about Shabbat. It means that the Jewish message is one of social justice—one of the great themes of the prophetic writings. In modern terms, Isaiah is challenging us to be role models to the world, by practicing what we preach and inspiring others.

According to the Torah, God has a very personal relationship with the Jewish people—so much so that God is furious over their continued oppression and exile in Babylonia. God promises to respond to their pain and to redeem them—to bring the Jews from all directions and restore them to their homeland of Israel.

Finally, God reminds the Judean exiles that God is, in fact, the only God: "I am the Lord, that is My name; I will not yield My glory to another, nor My renown to idols" (42:8). This is the major theological event in Second Isaiah—the "invention" of pure monotheism. Before that time, the Jews certainly believed in God, but the intense insistence of Second Isaiah that God is the only god was certainly unique for a time when the belief in polytheism (many gods) was still prevalent.

God needs the Jewish people to be God's "witnesses"—as if the entire world is a courtroom and the Jews are there to testify to God's uniqueness. Isaiah is in effect saying: "We are on a mission."

Every so often, a television station will feature a rerun of the movie *The Blues Brothers,* in which Dan Aykroyd and the late John Belushi play a pair of brothers, Jake and Elwood, who are blues singers. Elwood and Jake take on an important project: to save the Catholic orphanage in which they grew up from foreclosure. To quote Elwood: "We're on a mission from God."

The movie is a classic. So is Elwood's line about being on a mission from God. And, when you read this week's haftarah, you will notice something: the Jews invented the idea of being "on a mission from God." Second Isaiah puts it this way:

> I the Lord, in My grace, have summoned you,
> And I have grasped you by the hand.
> I created you, and appointed you
> A covenant people, a light of nations.
> Opening eyes deprived of light,
> Rescuing prisoners from confinement,
> From the dungeon those who sit in darkness. (42:6–7)

That is the clearest statement of the biblical concept that the Jews have a sacred mission. But what does that mission really entail?

Some of the prophet's words are easy to understand. God has a covenant with the Jewish people. They need to live up to that covenant by observing the commandments of the Torah. Many of these relate to doing justice. Isaiah calls upon us to rescue prisoners from their dungeons, to free those who are unjustly "imprisoned." In other words, to help the oppressed of the world.

The most famous phrase in the prophet's teaching, that the Jews are to be "a light of nations," has been the subject of much commentary. The medieval Spanish Jewish philosopher Rabbeinu Bachya understands it to mean that the Jews would need to be dispersed among the nations and that "it is the task of the Jews to teach the nations about God" (*Kad ha-Kemah*, 22). Claude Montefiore, a British Reform thinker, teaches: "Until the earth is filled with the knowledge of the One God—the God of Israel—the Jews will be his witnesses."

Most contemporary Jews agree that the phrase "a light of nations" means that Jews should teach the world about God and about ethics. Whenever Jews are involved in social justice, and influence others to do the same, that light shines brightly.

But perhaps "light to the nations" means something else as well. Throughout their history, the Jews have experienced much of the "darkness" of the world's hatred, culminating in the Holocaust. According to Israeli writer and statesman Avi Beker, "the Jews had to raise a light, and remind the world about the darkness of hatred that is still present." Like the Hanukkah candles, kindling light against the dark reminds us of our past history and our ongoing mission.

❖ Notes